Exmouth

You are
come

Activities to promote self-esteem and resilience in children from a diverse
community, including Asylum Seekers and Refugees

Pamela Allen, Ben Harper and Jay Rowell

Lucky Duck is more than a publishing house and training agency. George Robinson and Barbara Maines founded the company in the 1980s when they worked together as a head and psychologist developing innovative strategies to support challenging students.

They have an international reputation for their work on bullying, self-esteem, emotional literacy and many other subjects of interest to the world of education.

George and Barbara have set up a regular news-spot on the website. Twice yearly these items will be printed as a newsletter. If you would like to go on the mailing list to receive this then please contact us:

e-mail newsletter@luckyduck.co.uk   website www.luckyduck.co.uk

ISBN: 1 904 315 33 X

www.luckyduck.co.uk

Commissioning Editor: Barbara Maines
Editor: Mel Maines
Illustrators: Simon Smith, Marilyn Jones
Designer: Helen Weller
Cover: Barbara Maines

Printed in the UK by Antony Rowe Limited

Contents

Acknowledgements

After writing and piloting group work for asylum seeker and refugee young people in secondary schools in Sheffield I was approached by Ben Harper, a learning mentor in Sheffield, to consider piloting work with primary school aged asylum seeker and refugee children. I approached Jay Rowell (formerly Begum) who had collaborated with me on the previous work and we set about writing the sessions for the primary school version. After discussion and debate about the content of the programme we each went away and drafted two session plans each. From these rough session plans we approached primary schools. With the collaboration from the primary schools' learning mentors and the primary mental health workers in the Behaviour Education and Support Teams, Ben and I delivered, evaluated and redrafted the programme in line with the comments from the pupils and the facilitators.

From this process the programme was adapted for use with all primary school children and we would strongly encourage this. Discrimination and feeling different can take many forms. It is just as important to encourage white children to consider what it might feel like to be the outsider whilst also encouraging children to develop strategies that can help them bounce back from life's adversities. Racism breeds on ignorance and encouraging children's natural empathy may go someway in helping them to live a more enlightened future.

I would most like to thank the people who took part in the pilot of this programme, without whose commitment and contribution the work would not have evolved in the way that it has. I would particularly like to thank all the facilitators, David Hancock, Bright Sodje, Jasper Belgrave, Joanne Cooke and especially Dianne Bradshaw who has freely given her thoughts, comments and suggestions in such a positive and fun way.

I would also like to thank Gill Crow for her continued support and encouragement in all my work. My special thanks go to Ian Warwick for his belief and support in me always and his tireless encouragement and proofreading skills. I would like to acknowledge my own children Lauren and Tegan. I love them dearly. Both are at primary school and have great patience with me when I test ideas out on them. They never complain, even when I have brought my work home.

Finally and most importantly I would like to thank all the young people who took part in the pilot of the programme bringing it to life and engaging in the process whole heartedly, pupils from Park Hill Primary School, Pye Bank Primary School and Byron Wood Primary School, all in Sheffield. Thank you for being you.

Pam Allen

How to use the CD-ROM

The CD-ROM contains a PDF file labelled 'Worksheets.pdf' which contains worksheets for each session in this resource. You will need Acrobat Reader version 3 or higher to view and print these pages.

The document is set up to print to A4 but you can enlarge the pages to A3 by increasing the output percentage at the point of printing using the page set-up settings for your printer.

Alternatively, you can photocopy the worksheets directly from this book.

Foreword

Nearly 6.4 million people make up the black and minority ethnic population in England – 1 in 8 of the whole population. Their experience is characterised by disadvantage and discrimination (Making it Diverse, 2004).

Historically there has been an absence of effective strategies to deliver appropriate services to ethnic minority communities. Families are often offered services that are not appropriate or sensitive to their needs. This has often meant that black minority ethnic (BME) children, young people and their families come to services such as Child and Adolescent Mental Health Services (CAMHS) too late. As the Children's National Service Framework states. "...there is no convenient one size fits all."

The largest percentage of children and young people with mental health problems will be cared for outside of CAMHS provision and this is especially true for the majority of BME children and young people. Disparities and inequalities in terms of rates of mental ill health, service experience and service outcome are a major concern. Multi-agency and partnership working is therefore crucial if CAMHS and other agencies are going to address this imbalance.

By developing preventative strategies in partnership with other agencies and working in non-traditional settings some of these barriers may be slowly broken down. This may offer the chance for shared learning and understanding that could enhance the development of more appropriate services to these communities.

Reducing structural barriers to mental health and introducing policies which protect mental wellbeing will benefit everyone. Mental health promotion has some key principles, which include: reducing anxiety, enhancing control, facilitating participation and promoting social inclusion. These key principles are a close fit to the building blocks of resilience.

Considering racism as causative is an important step in developing a research agenda and responsive public services. This moves the discussion away from recruitment and access towards prevention and the impact of societal structures on the rates of illness. "Developing a deeper understanding of possible links between racism and health is a prerequisite for initiatives to decrease impact at a community and individual level," (McKenzie 2003). Equity of health cannot be achieved if one of the possible major causes of illness in minority ethnic groups does not have a dedicated research effort or preventative strategy.

The Green Paper 'Every Child Matters' (2003) targets the need to raise attainment of minority ethnic pupils by developing leadership capacity to deliver a whole-school approach to raising achievement; providing teachers with knowledge and skills; developing strategies to support bilingual learners; developing strategies for addressing low achievement of African-Caribbean students and decreasing exclusions. There is an opportunity for CAMHS tier two workers and Behaviour Education Support Team workers to collaborate on initiatives and develop preventative work around these issues, building self-esteem and raising the aspirations of BME young people. This group work programme may help in this process. If children and young people feel better supported emotionally then their capacity to learn will be increased and their chances of achieving greatly enhanced.

Developing emotional wellbeing and self-esteem would feed into local preventative strategies. Promoting positive mental health and emotional wellbeing and building self-esteem is a priority in the Children's National Service Framework. The Framework provides an opportunity to develop ways of working with BME children and young people and developing preventative work in partnership with schools, the youth service and others. This addresses the experience of BME children and young people and helps them engage in building up protective strategies.

The activities designed by Pamela Allen, Ben Harper and Jay Rowell are challenging and stimulating and go a long way to supporting children to achieve their full potential.

Ian Warwick

Senior Lecturer

University of Huddersfield

References

McKenzie, K. *Racism and Health.* 2003. BMJ 326: 65-66

DoH, Green Paper, 2003, *Every Child Matters*

DoH, *Getting the Right Start,* 2003, National Service Framework for Children, Emerging Findings

Radical Mentalities, Briefing Paper 3, 2004. *Making It Diverse.* Mental health promotion and black and minority ethnic groups. Mentality.

Introduction

This group work programme aims to provide some useful resources and practical activities to promote the emotional wellbeing and resilience of primary school children from diverse backgrounds.

Groups have provided a setting for personal change for many years and group work enables children and young people to understand themselves and how they interact with others. Groups can provide certain direct personal experiences unavailable through other methods and can be very valuable in personal education development or personal support. People in isolation can become trapped in their own negative views and beliefs. Sharing common experiences can often be a very empowering process. By listening to, and learning from other group members children and young people develop a greater sense of themselves. There are few environments where cultural minorities can be empowered to express and share perceptions. Group work is one of them.

Emotional literacy is the ability to recognise, understand and articulate feelings in relation to oneself and other people, and the capacity to develop constructive coping strategies to manage life's stresses. It is increasingly acknowledged that emotional literacy contributes to emotional wellbeing and can be promoted within schools. If a child is given insufficient emotional nurture this can lead to poor mental health.

Children and young people who are resilient have a number of protective factors. Such factors reside in the qualities of the young person, their families and their communities. Interpersonal and intra-personal protective factors such as self-esteem, sociability, autonomy, positive coping strategies, a positive attitude, a problem-solving approach, good communication skills and a capacity to reflect are all related to psychological resilience. Developing resilience does not mean that young people will become immune to stress but that they will be more likely to recover from negative events. Daniel et al (1999) identified three fundamental building blocks that underpin resilience:

1 a secure base, somewhere that the young person feels secure and belongs

2 good self-esteem, feeling competent and having an internal sense of worth

3 sense of self-efficacy, having an understanding of personal strengths and weaknesses and a sense of mastery and control.

Protective factors within the family are a reflection of patterns of family interaction that are warm, cohesive and supportive. Community protective factors are a reflection of the support and influence of peers and a feeling of support from an adult outside of the family.

It is hoped that this group work programme will allow children to:

▸ raise self-esteem

▸ improve listening skills

▸ increase insight and awareness

▸ build confidence

▸ enhance friendships

▸ develop individual coping strategies

▸ facilitate working together co-operatively

▸ offer understanding

▸ explore feelings

▸ have fun!

Evaluation

Some of the comments about the different group activities the children found most useful included, "Finding out the good things about us." Some children commented that they mostly enjoyed the activity which helped them to consider the good and bad things about being different.

Comments about the bad things about all being the same included:

"You wouldn't know who was who."
"You wouldn't know who was your friend."
"It will be boring."
"Everyone would be lost in a different family."

Some of the comments about what would be good if we were all the same included:

"There would be no teasing."
"Everyone would agree."
"There would be no racism."
"People would be kind, share, care and respect each other."

Definitions the children used to define 'asylum seeker' included:

"Different countries coming together to learn to be friends."
"People who go to new country to learn a new language."
"People coming from different countries because of war."

Definitions for 'refugee' included:

"People from poor countries to live in new house."
"Someone living in temporary housing."
"Someone who lives in old houses or flats."
"People from different countries."

Some children commented that they had enjoyed the activity 'A creature from another planet' the most.

"The helpful part was when we talked about the creature."

Comments about what the creature might think and feel about being new to this planet included:

- "lonely"
- "dispirited"
- "excited"
- "welcomed"
- "scared"
- "happy about new experience"
- "special"
- "sad about what has been left behind"
- "Other people would be scared, because of him being different"
- "If people helped the creature it would stop it feeling lonely"

They suggested ways to make the creature feel welcome:

- "show him around"
- "help him to read"
- "help him to write"
- "help him write his language"
- "teach him football"
- "talk to him"
- "help him with his work"
- "learn his language"

Some of the words they used to describe how it might feel to arrive on a different planet included:

- "hungry"
- "'frightened"
- "brave"
- "sad"

- "excited"
- "scared"
- "horrified"
- "shy"

The children also came up with lots of ideas about what the creature would be like, including, having special powers like 'mind reading' and would communicate by a colour code.

Words the participants used to describe the group included:

- "fantastic"
- "desirable"
- "fun and exciting"

- "excellent"
- "brilliant"
- "worthwhile"

Conclusion

Children need the resources to adapt successfully to changing physical, psychological and social environments. Where children are well resourced within themselves, within their family and social contexts, a capacity to constructively adapt to adversity or resilience can be promoted. This group work programme gives children an opportunity to begin building up their repertoire of coping in an empowering and supportive way.

Working within the school has two important advantages. It reduces stigma and develops the help-seeking behaviour of different cultural and minority ethnic groups. By normalising and de-stigmatising psychological support and providing it in settings already serving the minority ethnic population, contact is made with individuals who may otherwise be hard to reach. Building up relationships with parents or carers of the children is an important part of the process in developing trust and support and helps to embed the learning developed during the group work process.

Developing preventative group work in primary school settings opens up new ways of working. It can encourage children's and families use of external systems of support. It supports good mental health through a whole-school approach to the inclusion of all children from diverse backgrounds and the development of preventative strategies within the school. It reduces structural barriers to mental health services through initiatives to reduce discrimination and inequality and promotes access and inclusion.

All the children taking part in the pilot of the group work in Sheffield did not want the programme to end. They enjoyed working in a small group situation with adults who could give them time and attention and really wanted to know about their thoughts and feelings. The children felt valued, supported and listened to and from their comments found the group 'fun and worthwhile'.

References

Allen, P. (2002) *The Mental Health Needs Of Minority Ethnic Young People*, North Sheffield Young People's Mental Health Project, unpublished

Allen, P., Warwick, I. & Begum, J. (2004) *New in our Nation, Activities to promote self-esteem and resilience in young asylum seekers*, Lucky Duck Publishing, Bristol

Brandes, D. (1982) *Gamesters Handbook 2,* Teachers Edition, More games for teachers and group leaders, Cloth

Daniel, B., Wassell, S. & Gilligan, R. (1999) *Child Development for Child Care and Protection Workers*, Jessica Kingsley Publishers

Droust, J. & Bayley, S. (2001) *Therapeutic Groupwork with Children,* Speechmark Publishing

Hunt, H. (2002) *Feeling Special,* Emotional Literacy groupwork programme, unpublished

Sedgewick, J. (2002) *Parental Mental Illness* Groupwork Pack, North Sheffield Young People's Mental Health Project, unpublished

Sharp, P. (2001) *Nurturing Emotional Literacy, A Practical Guide for Teachers, Parents and those in the Caring Professions*, David Fulton Publishing

How to use the programme

At the beginning of the programme provide each young person with a folder to store the work safely. These will contain their evaluation forms, their affirmation cards and any other work they produce during the sessions. The sheets in each of the sessions should be photocopied from this book or, if you have access to a computer, they can be printed at a higher quality.

When an activity belongs to one particular session you will find it printed at the end of the session notes.

Each session includes notes for the facilitator which explain the aims and how to run the activities. At the end of each session there are three activities. These run throughout the programme:

1 Affirmations

2 Evaluation sheets

3 Reward stars

Affirmations

The affirmation cards are used for children to take away a positive thought to build on the learning from the group. It is useful if you can print out or photocopy the affirmations onto coloured card. The cards are laid out face up and the children are invited to choose a card and read the affirmation (with the help of the facilitator if needed). Initially children can find this activity challenging but over the course of the group, they begin to take on the meaning of the messages.

Evaluation sheets

The purpose of the evaluation sheet is for the children to have a voice in the process of the group. We believe that facilitators should be flexible and be able to adapt the programme to reflect the evaluation of the individuals taking part in the group. We very clearly stated to the children that we valued their honest assessment of the group and without their comments and contributions we would not have known what worked and what didn't. It was difficult for some of the children to be critical of the programme; this could be due to the strong relationships we built up within the group process. We found it helpful to remind the children what we had done during the session as they often forgot what we'd done at the beginning and therefore highlighted the last activity as their favourite. We also found it helpful to get the children to fill the forms out with the leading of a facilitator. This helps children to understand what they are being asked for, especially if literacy skills are an issue.

The evaluation serves to reinforce the benefits of being allowed to run group work within their school. Practitioners are increasingly being asked to provide evidence to justify their work. The evaluation serves as a tool to present arguments for being allowed to run groups. It also helps inform changes to the programme so that it evolves to meet the needs of future groups.

Reward stars

Reward stars are used at the end of each session to give the children a chance to assess how they think they have contributed and performed in the session. This activity should be done alone so that the children are not influenced by their peers. This activity serves as a way of monitoring any change in the children's self-esteem during the duration of the group work.

The programme follows the same format each week and also contains:

1 Check in

2 Icebreaker

3 Main activity

4 Trust game

5 Ending

Preparation

Arrange the room as you want it and display the poster for each session. You might want to use another copy of this on the door to indicate that a session is taking place and interruptions are discouraged.

Check in

The purpose of this is to ensure that the session starts with an opportunity for participants to share anything they may have thought about since the last session. We have also found that children respond far better to the activities when they understand why they are doing them. Sharing the aims with them at the beginning helps this process.

Icebreaker

Children may feel inhibited at first and the games can help break some of the barriers down. Having fun and creating energy in the group engages them in the work that follows. When playing the ABC of food, children often start the activity fairly reserved. Their imagination becomes stimulated as the activity progresses.

Main Activity

This varies from week to week and is the main focus of the sessions, enhancing resilience, self-esteem and empathy.

Trust game

Part of building self-esteem and community relies upon building the group from week to week. The trust games ask the children to disclose elements of themselves in a safe environment. Many children would find these activities difficult in isolation but within the safety of the group are able to practise trusting their peers.

Ending

This time is important in giving the children an opportunity to give immediate verbal feedback or comment on the session. It is also used to introduce the theme for the following session, which allows the children to give some thought to the topic before the next session.

Note

You will find the resources at the end of each section in which they are first used so for some activities used several times, such as affirmation cards, you can copy them for each subsequent session

▸ It is essential that each child be given a parental consent form, preferably in their mother tongue, before the beginning of the group so that parental permission is gained. It can be helpful to do home visits if resources allow (Appendix).

▸ If you are going to run a group within school it is advisable to select and interview the children before they take part in the group work.

- We recommend that the group is a closed group. Closed groups enable the establishment of a safe environment, with membership being decided at the beginning and not changing.

- It may also be necessary to modify the sessions to the time available. This pack has been written on the assumption that you will have an hour for the group.

- The group work as it is written is tailored to work with groups of between 8 and 12 young people. Individual activities may be suitable to run with smaller numbers including individuals. We have found the 'Creature from another planet' activity useful in groups looking at social skills and the 'Shield of strength' activity really beneficial when working with children on a one-to-one basis.

- The group work is planned for pupils in a primary school environment, 7 to 11 years old. We have found the programme works best with 9 to 11 year olds. Some extra support might be needed to help younger children benefit fully from the programme.

- Consider the needs of all participants. Icebreakers or trust games might need modifications for children with a disability or sensory impairment.

- You might want to address the language skills of the children before they participate in the course. This programme as it is written can only be used if the children have adequate English language skills. You should never use another child to interpret during the group work sessions.

- The issue of stability, safety and consistency are important factors in contributing to a successful group work programme. We would recommend that you use the same venue and room each week. We are aware that this can be difficult, especially in a busy school.

- Many activities take place in a round – sitting in a circle on chairs matched for height. The room should be suitable for this formation.

Session 1

Opening the group

Aims

▸ to introduce yourself, the participants and the aims of the group work programme

▸ to raise awareness of needs and responsibilities when working with others.

Plan for the session

1 Introduction

2 Icebreaker - Name game

3 Badge-making

4 Ground rules

5 Trust game

6 Affirmation cards

7 Ending the session

   evaluation

   reward stars

   plan for next session

   reassurance and continuity.

Materials

▸ Folder for each participant

▸ Poster - Welcome to our Group

▸ 'Aims of session' sheet

▸ Sticky labels or badge-making equipment

▸ Flip-chart and pens

▸ Selection of natural objects

▸ Affirmation cards

▸ Disposable camera

▸ Evaluation sheets

▸ Reward stars

Introduction

Arrange the room and display the poster.

It is important to clearly state the aims of the sessions. The underlying theme of this project is to raise self-esteem and resilience in children while allowing them to appreciate diversity within their own community.

This initial session is the most important in helping the children understand the benefits of being involved such as:

▸ gaining confidence and self-esteem

▸ developing strategies for coping and support

▸ developing relationship-building skills

▸ encouraging reflection.

You, as the facilitator, need to have a very clear and open mind when discussing some of the issues. It is imperative that the children continue to feel valued and respected and not marginalised and discriminated against. For example, it is important to stress the value of having an opportunity to think about their lives and to think about developing healthy ways to deal with stress. This can assist them to make the most of their opportunities.

It is important to stress to the children that no matter what their background or culture is, the skills that they learn may help them to deal with life's ups and downs. It is important to build-up trust and a safe environment within the group and give the children permission to be themselves.

In this programme we are going to deal with children as individuals; what they like and dislike, what kinds of things contribute to the way they are and who influences their choices.

The children might have strong feelings about these influences, positive or negative. These feelings can be explored with a view to supporting the group members in promoting the positive effects of these influences and reducing the negative effects. This programme will introduce many of these factors in stimulating and enjoyable activities.

Check in (3 mins)

Welcome the participants to the group and explain the purpose of the programme as stated above. State the aims of today's session.

Icebreaker - Name game (7 mins)

Introduce yourself. In a round ask each participant to introduce themselves and state something that they remember about their given names. It may be the meaning of the name. There may be a story about how the name was chosen, such as, "I was named after my grandmother." They may want to discuss whether they like their name or if they have any strong feelings about their name. This helps you and the participants to remember the names of all those involved in the group.

Badge-making session (15 mins)

All of the participants should write their names and draw a design on a label or a badge and wear it in the session. You can hire badge-making equipment or you can buy badge kits, similar to those used at conferences. If this is too expensive for your budget you can use sticky labels. It does help if the badges are worn for at least the first two or three sessions to help everyone to learn each other's name.

Ground rules (7 mins)

All group members should participate in developing the rules for the group, for example:

▸ Respect each other

▸ Listen to each other

▸ Be on time.

It is important that the group members agree procedures for absences: who to notify and how to make up the work they have missed.

The participants should be made to feel comfortable if they make a mistake or don't have the correct information or answers.

It may be helpful to begin by asking the participants what things they would not like to see in their group. You can then positively reframe these suggestions. For example, participants may say they do not want people interrupting and so this leads to a rule about listening.

The rules should be written on a piece of flip-chart paper and kept as a record for future sessions.

Trust game - Treasures (10 mins)

The participants should sit in a circle. Lay out a selection of natural objects, for example shells, beads, wood and any other treasures.

Ask the participants to choose an object and then explain to the group the reason they choose the object - what it reminds them of, how it feels, what it looks like and anything they have noticed about the object since they looked at it.

Affirmation cards (4 mins)

Lay out a selection of affirmation cards for the participants to choose from.

Each participant reads their chosen card out to the rest of the group. Some participants may need help with the reading.

This enables them to take away a positive thought from the session. The card can then be put in their folders as a reminder of their positive qualities.

Ending the session (4 mins)

1   As the session ends, give participants the opportunity to ask any questions they may have about the group and today's session.

2   Mention the plan for the next session, "Next session we will be looking at the kinds of things we like and dislike and what kinds of things might influence us in our choices about how we view ourselves in the world. There are lots of things that influence and describe who we are and we will look at a few examples of these next week. It would be useful if you could think about some of these things before we meet again."

3   Hand out the disposable cameras and ask participants to take photographs of all the things that are important to them, for example, family, friends, pets, home, a favourite place, a favourite item. The participants are asked to bring back the used camera for the following week in order for the photographs to be developed for the third session. If there is no budget to buy disposable cameras, the participants are asked to collect any items that they could use for a collage from home, the community or school. They could collect things from magazines or draw items that are important to them.

4   Collect in the name badges to be distributed in next week's session.

Evaluation (5 mins)

Hand out the evaluation forms to each participant.

Read through each section of the sheet with the participants and ask them to fill it in, helping them to reflect on the session. Some participants may need help in writing.

This form goes into the participant's folder. Make an extra copy for you to evaluate the group work at the end of the programme.

Reward stars (5 mins)

As participants leave the room, they are asked to choose whether they want to take two, four or six stars that reflect their performance in the group.

You may say, "You can choose to take two, four or six stars for your involvement in today's session. How many do you think you deserve or would like?" Participants then take whatever they ask for and you record the information each week for each individual child as a way of monitoring their progress.

It is important that this is done away from the main group so that peers do not influence each other.

Welcome to our Group

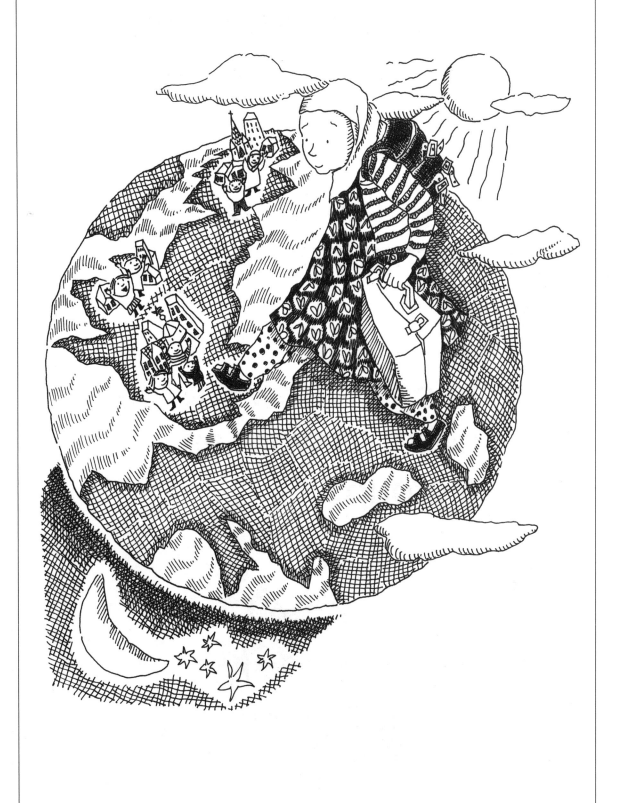

Aims

▶ **to understand what our group is about**

▶ **to get to know each other**

▶ **to agree how we are going to work as a group.**

Affirmation cards

I have happy thoughts	I am calm
I am generous	I am kind
I am strong	I trust my feelings
I am able to forgive others	All I have to do is believe
I can	I am cool

Affirmation Cards

I am great

I think of others

I do the best with what I have

I can forgive myself

I have choices

I am in control

I can give and accept
help in my life

I look after myself

I am kind to myself

I am thoughtful

Affirmation Cards

I am helpful

I choose friends who bring out the best in me

If I keep trying I can

I am thoughtful

I choose to be strong for myself

I am brave enough to face the future

I have the courage to make things work

I am creative

I am supportive

I can do anything I want if I put my mind to it

Session 1 - Evaluation

How much have you enjoyed the session? (Please circle)

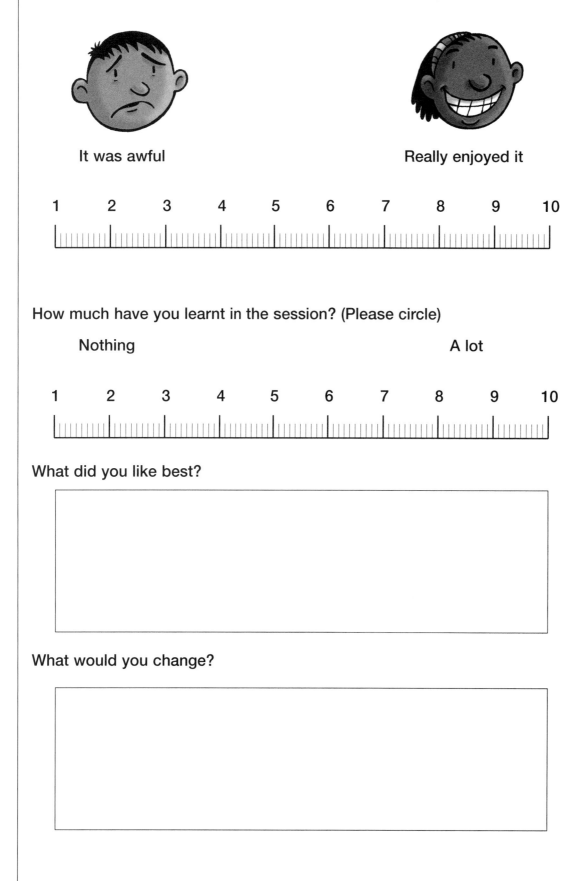

It was awful

Really enjoyed it

1   2   3   4   5   6   7   8   9   10

How much have you learnt in the session? (Please circle)

Nothing

A lot

1   2   3   4   5   6   7   8   9   10

What did you like best?

What would you change?

Reward Stars

Session 2
Who we are

Aims

▸ to promote awareness of factors that influence the way we feel about ourselves

▸ to introduce concepts of how we see ourselves in the world, our likes and dislikes

▸ to explore how society might judge us because of our looks, our image, our culture and our diversity

▸ to think about how we can help young people to understand the different definitions that we have in society to describe people because of their race, culture, status, disability or gender.

Plan for the session

1 Check in

2 Icebreaker - Pass the name

3 Picture taking

4 Definitions - Pass the parcel or Stories

5 Trust game - Two truths and a lie

6 Ending the session

   information about the next session

   evaluation

   affirmation cards

   reward stars.

Materials

▸ 'Aims of session' sheet

▸ Poster - Picture of Fatima and Ahmed

▸ Name badges

▸ Ball

▸ 'Introducing me' sheet

▸ Digital or Polaroid camera and film

▸ Tape recorder and music

▸ Parcel with definitions and a sweet enclosed in every layer

▸ Flip-chart, paper, pens, felt tips, coloured pencils

▸ Definition and story of asylum seeker and refugee

▸ Affirmation cards (from Session 1)

▸ Evaluation sheet

▸ Reward stars (from Session 1).

Check in (2 mins)

Arrange the room and display the poster.

Welcome back the participants and give out the name badges.

Collect the disposable cameras in from last week.

Reintroduce the ground rules and ask the participants if they have anything that they would like to add.

Give time for anyone to raise any issues from the last session and state the aims of today's session.

Icebreaker - Pass the name (5 mins)

Invite participants to sit in a circle. One of the participants throws a ball to another participant whilst saying the name of the participant who catches the ball.

On catching the ball, participants are encouraged to look at the person who threw the ball and say, "Thank you."

If the participants can speak more than one language you could encourage the participants to say thank you in another language or their mother tongue.

The person with the ball now repeats the process.

(Monitor this game to make sure that nobody is left out.)

Introducing me (15 mins)

Give the participants the 'Introducing me' sheet to complete.

With prior permission from the group take a Polaroid or digital photograph of each participant.

Once dry or printed off the participants can glue their photograph onto their 'Introducing me' sheet.

You may need to assist some participants with filling in the writing element on the sheet.

Participants are invited to share their work with each other.

Definitions - Pass the parcel (15 mins)

Prepare a parcel with several layers of paper. In each layer place a piece of coloured paper printed with one of the definitions and a wrapped sweet. Make enough layers so that each participant has a turn.

Put the music on and pass the parcel around the group. When the music stops the participant holding the parcel opens one layer and wins the sweet and tells the group the word that is enclosed in that layer of the parcel.

Encourage the group to discuss the term.

- ▶ What does it mean to them?
- ▶ Are there any other words that describe the same thing?
- ▶ Do people make assumptions about certain definitions?
- ▶ What kind of assumptions might these be?
- ▶ Can these assumptions be hurtful?
- ▶ Do they really describe who the person is who is given these labels?

For example, a participant may find the term 'racism' in the parcel. The participants may then say, "This is when someone says something hurtful about their skin colour." You can help the participants to expand on this by asking for any real life examples that they might have witnessed or experienced. Continue by asking whether the name called is accurate and factual or whether it refers to things that happen to a person.

Write the participants comments onto flip-chart paper.

Put the music on again and repeat the process until all the definitions have gone or all the participants have opened up the parcel at least once.

Alternative definitions activity for use with asylum seeker or refugee participants (15 mins)

Put the terms 'refugee' and 'asylum seeker' onto flip-chart paper. Ask participants to brainstorm what each word means to them, to society, to friends and so on. Are there any other words used to describe these terms?

Show the group Fatima's picture and read the accompanying story about her going through the asylum seeking process. Then show the group Ahmed's picture and read the accompanying story of his gaining refugee status.

Share with the participants the definitions of 'asylum seeker' and 'refugee' and invite participants to comment. Explain that the terms refer to a process that someone who is seeking safety, security and stability has to go through in order to remain in the country they have arrived in.

The definitions of asylum seeker and refugee can be used as a poster for the group session and as a handout for the participants to keep in their folders.

Trust game - Two truths and a lie (8 mins)

Each participant makes 3 statements about themselves; 2 are true and 1 is a lie. The other participants have to guess which one is the lie.

Affirmation cards (4 mins)

Lay out a selection of affirmation cards for the participants to choose from. Each participant reads their chosen card out to the rest of the group. Some participants may need help with reading.

The participants are encouraged to take the card home as a reminder of their positive qualities and keep in their group work folder.

Ending (1 min)

1   As the session ends, give participants the opportunity to ask any questions they may have about the group and today's session.

2   Mention briefly what the contents of the following week's session will contain. "Next week we will be making a collage using the photographs you have taken during the last week. You can also bring in any additional materials you may want to use on your collage, which will help to demonstrate who you are and the kinds of things you like."

3   Collect in the name badges to distribute out in the next session.

Evaluation (5 mins)

Hand out evaluation forms to each participant.

Read through each section of the sheet with the participants and ask them to fill it in, helping them to reflect on the session.

Some participants may need help in writing.

Reward stars (5 mins)

As in Session 1, the participants are asked to choose whether they want to take two, four or six stars that reflect their performance in the group.

Aims

▶ **to explore what makes us who we are**

▶ **to understand differences between us.**

Fatima

Ahmed

Introducing me...

My Picture

My name is

I am

years old.

I was born in

I like

I don't like

This was an important day for me

Asylum Seeker

Fatima was eight years old when she had to leave Somalia.

"I came back from school and remember seeing our house had collapsed. Only bits of it were remaining. Then I saw tanks in front of our house and they began firing. It was terrible. I was very scared.

There was a lot of fear around. Things got so bad that we couldn't even go to school or play out anywhere.

Me and my mum escaped to Africa where we stayed until we got enough money to buy a ticket to England. Some of our relatives lived in London.

When we got here we got a temporary house, which we are allowed to stay in until the authorities have decided whether we can stay here forever or we have to go back to Somalia.

I miss some of my old friends and family but hope we can stay here because I feel safer and I can go to school."

Refugee

Ahmed was five years old when he had to leave Afghanistan.

"When I was small I was happy. People were nice to me and I loved my school.

One night some men came to our house and took my father away and we have not seen him since. It makes me feel sad when I think about it.

My mum decided we had to leave Afghanistan because it wasn't safe for us anymore. We came to Britain and we were given a house to stay in and I started a new school.

The authorities have said we can stay here for good because Afghanistan would not be a safe place for our family to go back to.

I still miss my dad but I like my new school and my new friends. My mum goes to college and is learning English. She would like to help other families who are new to our area."

Definitions

Refugee

▸ Is someone who feels that where they were born is not a safe place to live. They have gone to another country and that country has agreed that they can stay in order to be safe.

Asylum Seeker

▸ Is someone who has had to leave the country where they were born. They have gone to another country to be safe and asked them if they can stay. They are waiting for that country to say it is okay and then they will have refugee status.

Definitions

Refugee

- Is someone who feels that where they were born is not a safe place to live. They have gone to another country and that country has agreed that they can stay in order to be safe.

Asylum Seeker

- Is someone who has had to leave the country where they were born. They have gone to another country to be safe and asked them if they can stay. They are waiting for that country to say it is okay and then they will have refugee status.

Mixed race

- This refers to the fact that your mother and father come from different races. People from different parts of the world are said to be from different races.

Racism

- Racism is saying or doing something to hurt someone who comes from a different culture.

Discrimination

- This is when people are treated differently because they belong to a certain group.

Sexism

- This is when girls or women are treated unfairly.

Stereotyping

- This is when people make assumptions about a person. For instance: all boys are tough or all girls like Barbie dolls.

Session 2 - Evaluation

How much have you enjoyed the session? (Please circle)

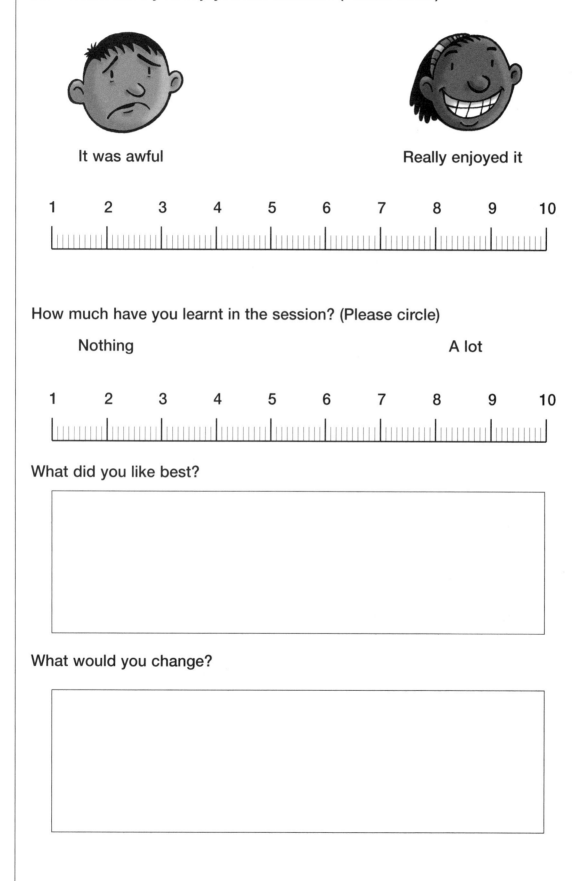

It was awful

Really enjoyed it

1   2   3   4   5   6   7   8   9   10

How much have you learnt in the session? (Please circle)

Nothing

A lot

1   2   3   4   5   6   7   8   9   10

What did you like best?

What would you change?

Session 3
Important things to me

Aims

▸ to celebrate, explore and create a collage of memories, experiences and events

▸ to support participants to communicate creatively many different aspects of their life

▸ to create a piece of artwork that will identify and recognise important people, places and things in their life.

Plan for the session

1 Check in

2 Icebreaker - The ABC of food

3 Collage

4 Trust game - Sad tears and happy tears

5 Ending the session

> information about the next session
>
> evaluation
>
> affirmation cards
>
> reward stars.

Materials

▸ Name badges

▸ Posters - Sad tear and Happy tear

▸ 'Aims of session' sheet

▸ ABC of food list

▸ Photographs from disposable cameras

▸ Coloured paper or card, marker pens, pencil crayons

▸ Maps, flags, travel brochures, catalogues, felt material

▸ Leaves, feathers, twigs, wood shavings

▸ Sequins, string, glitter pens, glue, sellotape

▸ Affirmation cards (from Session 1)

▸ Evaluation sheet

▸ Reward stars (from Session 1).

Check in (2 mins)

Arrange the room and display the posters.

Welcome back the group. Give out the name badges to participants.

Give time for anyone to raise any issues from the last session and state the aims for this session.

Icebreaker - The ABC of food (6 mins)

Sit the participants in a circle. A person is chosen to go first and must think of and tell the group a food beginning with the letter 'A'.

The next person must do the same with the letter 'B' and so on throughout the alphabet.

You may need to help the participants if they are having difficulties with certain letters of the alphabet. A prompt sheet has been provided to help you with this. It is okay to pass on some letters of the alphabet and move straight onto the next letter.

Collage (30 mins)

Give each participant a large piece of paper or card and invite them to create a collage using materials provided, any materials from home and their photographs, which they took between Session 1 and 2.

The collage will represent the things that are important to the individual including people, places, events, hobbies and other things they like.

It is important that you encourage, assist and support the participants throughout this activity.

At the end of the activity, participants are invited to share their work with the rest of the group.

Trust game - Sad tears and happy tears (7 mins)

Sit the participants in a circle and pass an image of a sad tear around the circle.

Encourage group members to share something that has made them feel sad. It might be the death of a grandparent or pet, or maybe falling out with a friend or upsetting someone. It might be that they lost a favourite possession or didn't get picked to play a game.

It is important to give a range of options to the participants so they know they do not have to share very painful memories if they do not want to. It is okay to share with the group something that just made you feel a bit sad or disappointed.

It is helpful if the facilitator starts this activity to encourage safe and appropriate responses.

An image of a happy tear is passed around the circle and participants are encouraged to share something that has made them very happy. Again it may be helpful for you to start the round.

With both tears, participants should be able to pass if they do not want to answer.

Affirmation cards (4 mins)

Lay out a selection of affirmation cards for the participants to choose from.

Each participant reads their chosen card out to the rest of the group. Some participants may need help with reading.

Encourage participants to take cards home as a reminder of their positive qualities.

Ending (1 min)

1   As the session ends, give participants the opportunity to ask any questions they may have about the group and today's session.

2   Mention briefly what the contents of the following week's session will contain. "Next

week we will look at the advantages and disadvantages of people being different and we will also look at the kinds of things that make us unique and individual."

3 Collect in the name badges to use again in next week's session.

Evaluation (5 mins)

Hand out the evaluation form to each participant.

Read through each section of the sheet with the participants and ask them to fill it in, helping them to reflect on the session.

Some participants may need help in writing.

Reward stars (5 mins)

As participants leave the room, they choose whether they want to take two, four or six stars that reflect their performance in this session.

Aim

▶ **to identify and celebrate the important people, places and things in our lives.**

ABC of food

A - apple, avocado, apricot, almond, Alpen

B - bacon, beans, broccoli, banana, butter, biscuit, bread, bun, bhajis

C - cabbage, cauliflower, carrot, cake, cookie, crisps, courgette, cheese, custard, cereal, chips, chapati

D - donut, damson, dip, dumpling, duck, dahl, dhansak

E - Edam cheese, eggs, escalopes

F - fish, fromage frais, fudge

G - goose, grapes, grapefruit, guacamole, gummy bears, gobstopper, goulash

H - hummus, halibut, haddock, ham

I - ice-cream, icing, Iceberg lettuce

J - jam, jalfrezi, jelly, jammy dodgers, jaffa cakes, jerk chicken

K - kangaroo, kolfie, kippers, king prawn, korma, kumquats

L - lettuce, lamb, lemon, lime, lolly, liver

M - meat, mussels, meringue, melon

N - nachos, naan bread, nuts

O - orange, oats, offal, octopus, olives, oil

P - peas, porridge, potato, peach, passion fruit, pomegranate, pancake

Q - quail, quorn, quince, quiche

R - raisins, rhubarb, rice, ravioli, rabbits, ricotta,

S - sausage, star fruit, soup, spring rolls, spaghetti, spinach, sagaloo

T - toast, tomato, treacle, toffee

U - ugly fruit, um bongo

V - veal, venison, vegetable, vindaloo

W - watercress, watermelon, white bait, waffle, weetabix

X - extra helpings!

Y - yoghurt, yams

Z - zabaglione.

43

Happy tear

Sad tear

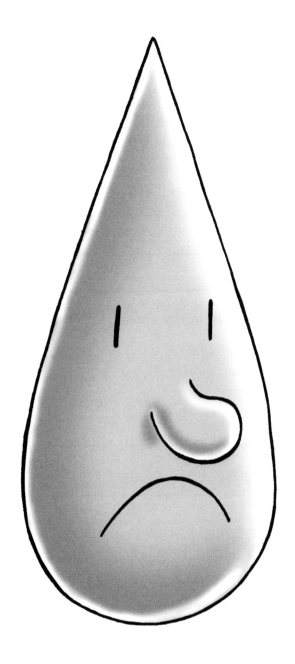

Session 3 - Evaluation

How much have you enjoyed the session? (Please circle)

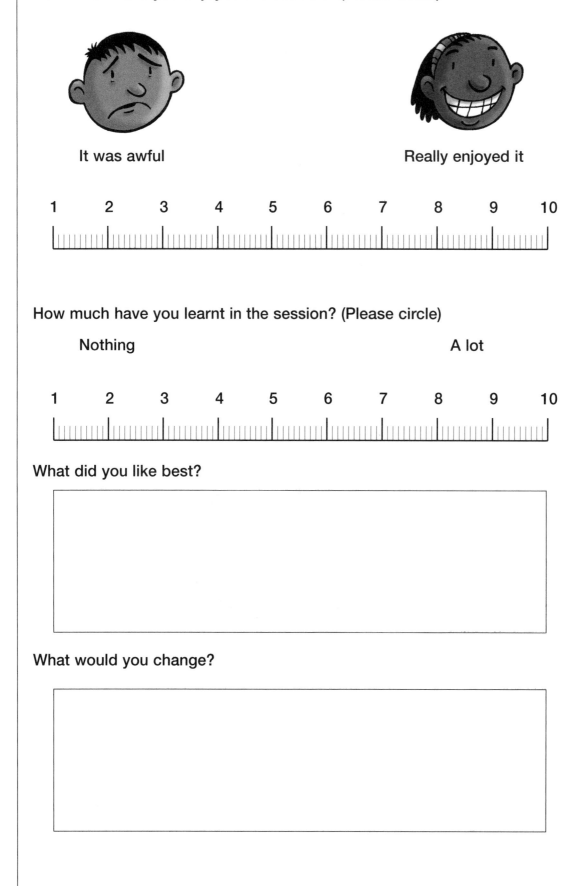

It was awful   Really enjoyed it

1   2   3   4   5   6   7   8   9   10

How much have you learnt in the session? (Please circle)

Nothing   A lot

1   2   3   4   5   6   7   8   9   10

What did you like best?

What would you change?

Session 4
Similarities and differences

Aims

▶ for participants to understand that everyone has strengths, weaknesses, similarities and differences

▶ to appreciate the richness of cultures and experiences that exist in society.

Plan for the session

1 Check in

2 Icebreaker - Secret whispers

3 Good and bad things about difference

4 Great things about...

5 Trust game - Rhythmic clapping

6 Ending the session

   information about the next session

   evaluation

   affirmation cards

   reward stars.

Materials

▶ Name badges

▶ Poster - We are all the Same

▶ 'Aims of session' sheet

▶ Pens

▶ 'Good things' sheet

▶ 'Bad things' sheet

▶ 'Great things about' sheet

▶ Affirmation cards (from Session 1)

▶ Evaluation sheet

▶ Reward stars (from Session 1).

Check in (2 mins)

Arrange the room and display the poster.

Welcome back the group. Give out the name badges to participants and make time for anyone to raise any issues from the last session and state the aims of this session.

Icebreaker - Secret whispers (8 mins)

Participants sit in a circle. Someone is chosen to whisper a phrase to the person on his or her left.

They are only allowed to whisper the phrase once.

What the listener hears must be whispered to the next person in the circle and so on until it comes to the last person.

After the last person has been whispered to, they must say out loud what they have heard.

The fun is in comparing what the original phrase was with what the final person quotes!

Good and bad things about difference (10 mins)

Ask the participants to sit in a circle and explain that in many ways we are different from each other and in other ways we are similar to each other.

Show the poster 'We are all the same' and split the group up into two.

Ask one group to brainstorm all the advantages about being the same and give them the 'Good things' sheet to record their answers on.

Ask the other group to brainstorm all the disadvantages and record their answers on the 'Bad things' sheet.

Once this task has been completed ask the participants to gather back into the bigger group and discuss and share what they have written.

It is important for you to support participants in the small group work, especially with the written element.

This activity can also be done as a whole-group exercise.

Great things about... (20 mins)

Prepare the 'Great things about...' sheet with a named page for each member of the group.

Split the group into two. Each group has the task of brainstorming all the great things about members of the other group.

The group members all write down the positive qualities of each member of the other group in turn, ensuring that each child has a completed a 'Great things about' sheet.

Ask participants to present their sheets to each other.

Every participant should take away a sheet with positive comments about themselves, generated by the other group members.

The group come back together and discuss how they feel receiving such positive comments.

Trust game - Rhythmic clapping game (5 mins)

Ask the participants to sit in a circle.

Ask for a volunteer to start the game by clapping or gesturing in a certain way.

The person on the left repeats the clap or gesture and adds their own, for example, they may clap their hands and then snap their fingers.

All the participants need to imitate what the previous participants have done as well as add their own. Eventually there will be a chain of different claps or gestures going around the group.

Different features could include: snapping fingers with both hands or one hand, stamping feet, clapping your hands a different number of times, slapping the sides of your legs and so on.

Affirmation cards (4 mins)

Lay out a selection of affirmation cards for the participants to choose from.

Each participant reads their chosen card out to the rest of the group.

Some participants may need help with reading.

Encourage participants to take the cards home as a reminder of their positive qualities.

Ending (1 min)

1   As the session ends, give participants the opportunity to ask any questions they may have about the group and today's session.

2   Mention briefly what the contents of the following week's session will contain. "Next week we will look at how it feels to be different or new."

3   Collect in the name badges to give out in next week's session.

Evaluation (5 mins)

Hand out the evaluation form to each participant.

Read through each section of the sheet with the participants and ask them to fill it in, helping them to reflect on the session.

Some participants may need help in writing.

Reward stars (5 mins)

As participants leave the room, ask them to choose whether they want to take 2, 4 or 6 stars that reflect their performance in the group.

Aims

▶   **to look at the good and bad things about being different**

▶   **to think about the good things about us.**

We are all the Same

Good things about being different

Bad things about being different

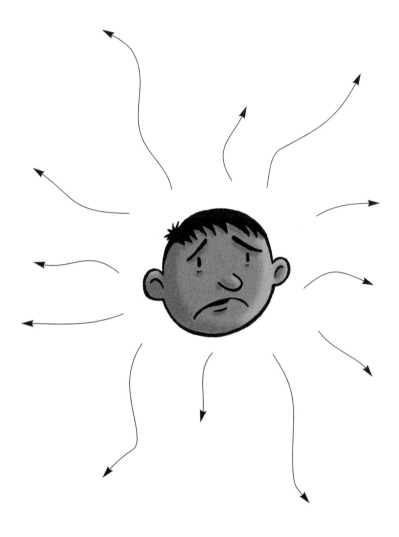

Great things about...

Session 4 - Evaluation

How much have you enjoyed the session? (Please circle)

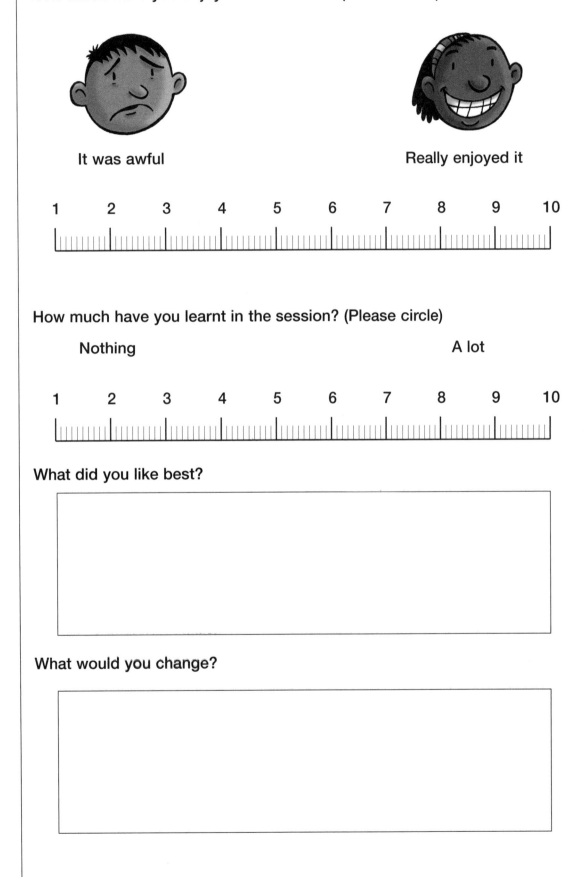

It was awful

Really enjoyed it

| 1 | 2 | 3 | 4 | 5 | 6 | 7 | 8 | 9 | 10 |

How much have you learnt in the session? (Please circle)

Nothing

A lot

| 1 | 2 | 3 | 4 | 5 | 6 | 7 | 8 | 9 | 10 |

What did you like best?

What would you change?

Session 5

What is it like to be different?

Aim

▸ to promote empathy and social skills

▸ to use a safe activity for children to express their feelings about being different or new.

Plan for the session

1 Check in

2 Icebreaker - Fruit salad

3 A creature from another planet

4 Trust game - Catch me

5 Ending the session

information about the next session

evaluation

affirmation cards

reward stars.

Materials

▸ Name badges

▸ Poster - Creature from Another Planet

▸ 'Aims of session' sheet

▸ Flip-chart paper and pens

▸ Affirmations (from Session 1)

▸ Evaluation sheet

▸ Reward stars (from Session 1).

Check in (2 mins)

Arrange the room and display the poster.

Welcome back the group and give out the name badges.

Give time for anyone to raise any issues from the last session and state the aims of this session.

Icebreaker - Fruit salad (5 mins)

With the group members sitting in a circle label each participant one of three fruits.

In turn, call out one of the three fruits and the participants who have been given the name of that particular fruit has to change places.

To add more to the fun, you could call two fruits at a time.

When fruit salad is called, everyone changes places.

A creature from another planet (30 mins)

Show the participants the image of a creature from another planet and generate a discussion about the creature by asking a series of questions as below:

- ▸ What do you think the creature is named?
- ▸ How old do you think the creature is?
- ▸ Where do you think the creature comes from?
- ▸ Can you describe what the creature's planet is like?
- ▸ What do you think the creature eats?
- ▸ Do you think the creature has any family?
- ▸ How do you think the creature communicates?
- ▸ Do you think the creature might be lonely on our planet?
- ▸ Do you think the creature will make friends easily?
- ▸ How do you think other children would treat the creature?
- ▸ How do you think adults would treat the creature?
- ▸ How do you think people would treat the creature when it first arrived, do you think this might change, what kinds of things might change people's attitudes to the creature?
- ▸ How would you make this creature feel welcome?

Ask the participants to think about being a creature from another planet and to think about words to describe how they might feel if they arrived on a strange new planet.

It is important that you write down all the participants' ideas onto flip chart paper.

Trust game - Catch me (8 mins)

Ask for a volunteer to join you in the middle of a circle.

Ask the participant to trust you and standing with legs together and knees straight, fall back into your arms.

Participants are then invited one by one to repeat the activity.

Some participants may want to help you to catch others.

Affirmation cards (4 mins)

Lay out a selection of affirmation cards for the participants to choose from.

Each participant reads their chosen card out to the rest of the group. Some participants may need help with reading.

Encourage participants to take the cards home as a reminder of their positive qualities.

Ending (1 min)

1. As the session ends, give the participants the opportunity to ask any questions they may have about the group and today's session.

2. Mention briefly what the contents of the following week's session will contain. "Next week we will look at the things that make us feel strong and supported and we will make a shield that reflects this. It will be helpful if you begin to think about the things that are important to you and that give you strength."

3. Collects in the name badges to distribute in next weeks session.

Evaluation (5 mins)

Hand out the evaluation form to each participant.

Read through each section of the sheet with the participants and ask them to fill it in, helping them to reflect on the session.

Some participants may need help in writing.

Reward stars (5 mins)

As participants leave the room, ask them to choose whether they want to take two, four or six stars that reflect their performance in the group.

Creature from Another Planet

Aim

▶ **to understand how others may feel about being different or new and how we can help them.**

Session 5 - Evaluation

How much have you enjoyed the session? (Please circle)

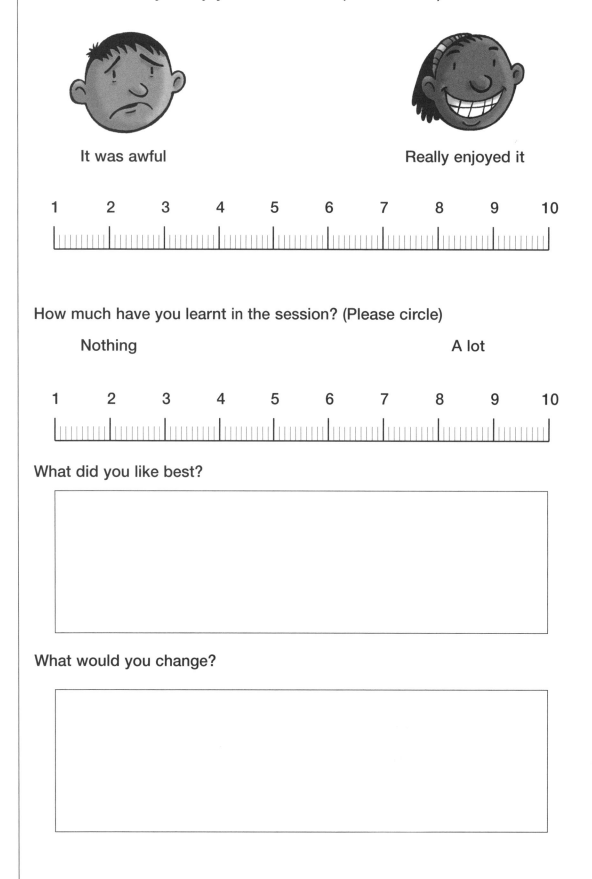

It was awful

Really enjoyed it

1   2   3   4   5   6   7   8   9   10

How much have you learnt in the session? (Please circle)

Nothing

A lot

1   2   3   4   5   6   7   8   9   10

What did you like best?

What would you change?

Session 6
My shield of strength

Aims

▶ to help participants explore systems of support available to them

▶ to help participants build up a picture of their individual coping strategies and identity

▶ to build up a personal profile in visual collage form of all the things that they find helpful and protective in their lives.

Plan for the session

1 Check in

2 Icebreaker - Silent statements

3 My shield of strength

4 Trust game - Saying goodbye

5 Ending the session

    information about the next session

    evaluation

    affirmation cards

    reward stars.

Materials

▶ Name badges

▶ Poster - Shield of Strength

▶ 'Aims of session' sheet

▶ Shield shapes on large card

▶ Coloured paper, card, marker pens, pencil, crayons

▶ Travel brochures, catalogues

▶ Ball of string or wool

▶ Leaves, feathers, twigs, felt material, wood shavings

▶ Sequins, string, glitter pens, glue, sellotape

▶ Affirmation cards (from Session 1)

▶ Evaluation sheets

▶ Certificate of completion

▶ Reward stars (from Session 1).

Check in (2 mins)

Arrange the room and display the poster.

Welcome the group members back and give time for anyone to raise any issues from the last session. State the aims of this session.

Icebreaker - Silent statements (5 mins)

Ask participants to sit in a circle. Begin by making a statement, which may or may not apply to some or all of the participants.

Any participant whom the statement applies to has to change places.

For example, all those wearing blue socks have to change places or all those who watched Eastenders last night have to change places if this statement applies to them.

Ask the participants to suggest their own statements.

My shield of strength (30 mins)

Ask the participants to think about all the different ways of protecting themselves against feeling hurt, the things that make themselves feel good about themselves and the things that mean a lot to them.

Give out the shield shapes. You can either cut them out on large pieces of card or blow up the template onto A3 size paper. Hand out the craft materials and magazines. Ask the participants to fill in the sections on the shield. They can use the sections as a guide to think about their own coping skills, their main supports and their wish for the future.

> This is where I feel safe
>
> These are the people I trust
>
> These are the things I most enjoy
>
> If I had one wish I would wish for...

Participants may need encouragement to think about what they will put in each section before they start to decorate the shield itself. Ask the group members to write, paint, draw or find images to build up their own personal 'coat of arms'. Go around and help them to fill in their shield.

Trust game - Saying goodbye (8 mins)

Ask the participants to sit in a circle with one member holding a ball of string or wool.

The participant with the ball of string looks around and says goodbye and a final message to one of the other participants. Holding on to the end of the string they throw the string to the participant they said the goodbye to.

The person who receives the string then repeats the process.

This carries on until everyone has said goodbye.

At the end there is silence and the facilitator then cuts all the string that is now criss-crossing the circle, symbolising the end of the group.

Participants are encouraged to keep their piece of string to remind them of the group.

Affirmation cards (4 mins)

Lay out a selection of affirmation cards for the participants to choose from.

Each participant reads their chosen card out to the rest of the group. Some participants may need help with reading.

Encourage participants to take cards home as a reminder of their positive qualities.

Ending (1 min)

As the session ends, give the participants the opportunity to ask any questions they may have about the group and today's session.

Evaluation (5 mins)

Hand out the evaluation forms to each participant, one for the individual session and one for the group as a whole. Ask the participants to include their thoughts about the things that they liked most during the group and the things they liked least.

Read through each section of the sheet with the participants and ask them to fill it in, helping them to reflect on the session.

Some participants may need help in writing.

Give out certificates for the completion of the programme.

Reward stars (5 mins)

As participants leave the room, ask them to choose whether they want to take 2, 4 or 6 stars that reflect their performance in the group.

Aim

▶ **to look at the things that make us feel strong and safe.**

My Shield of Strength

This is where I feel safe

These are the people I trust

These are the things I most enjoy

If I had one wish it would be for…

Session 6 - Evaluation

How much have you enjoyed the session? (Please circle)

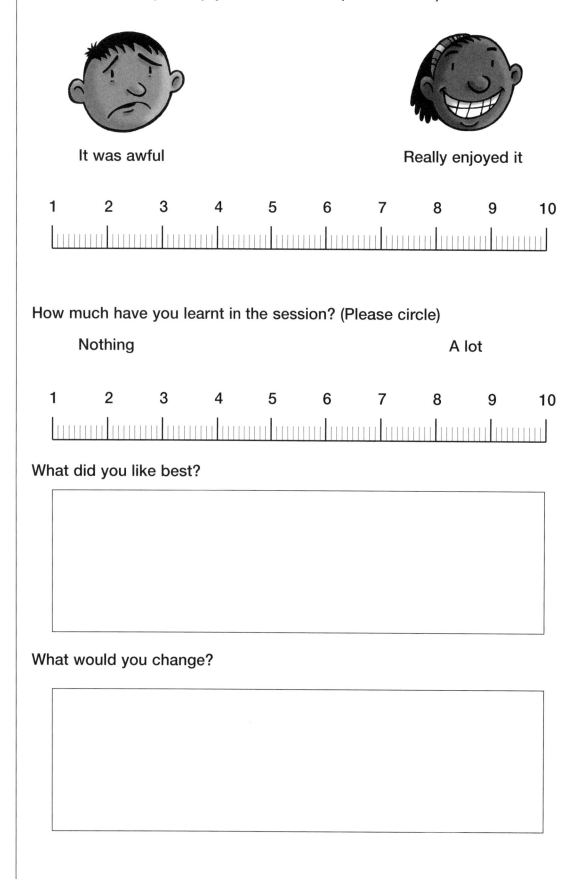

It was awful

Really enjoyed it

1   2   3   4   5   6   7   8   9   10

How much have you learnt in the session? (Please circle)

Nothing

A lot

1   2   3   4   5   6   7   8   9   10

What did you like best?

What would you change?

Certificate

Thank you for joining us
We wish you well

Name

Has participated in
a course to welcome
new arrivals in
our nation

Signed _____   **Date** _____

Overall Evaluation

How much have you enjoyed the sessions? (Please circle)

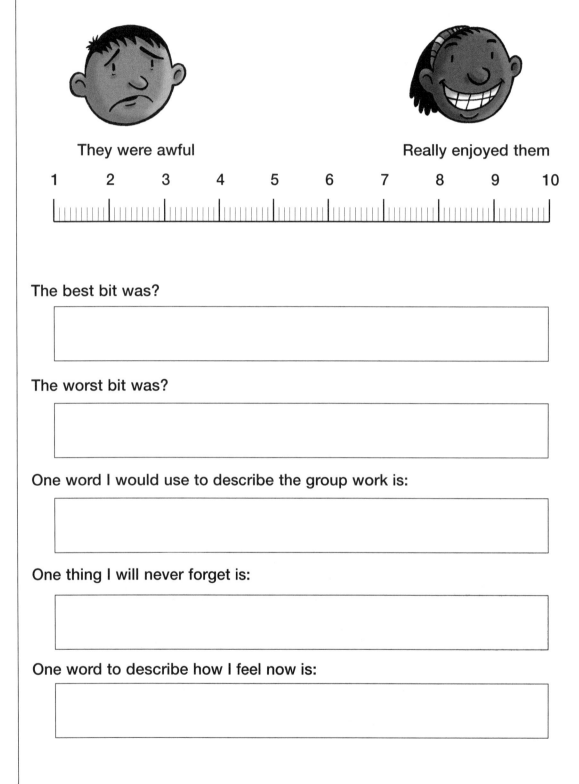

They were awful   Really enjoyed them

1   2   3   4   5   6   7   8   9   10

The best bit was?

The worst bit was?

One word I would use to describe the group work is:

One thing I will never forget is:

One word to describe how I feel now is:

Appendix

Example of a Parental Consent Letter

Dear Parent/Carer

As part of the school's aim to help build up confidence and raise self-esteem, I am pleased to be able to tell you that your child has been given the opportunity to participate in a six week group work programme.

The group will take place every ....at ....until.............

It will involve building teamwork skills, raising self-esteem and confidence building.

If you are happy for your child to participate in this group work programme, please fill in and sign the consent slip below and return it to.......................................

by.......................................

Yours faithfully

Example of a reply slip

I give permission for my child to participate in the six week group work programme.

I understand that the group work sessions will take place every.................................

at................until...................

Name of Pupil... Form/Class.................................

Signature of Parent/Carer: _____

Don't forget to visit our website for all our latest publications, news and reviews.

www.luckyduck.co.uk

New publications every year on our specialist topics:

- ▸ **Emotional Literacy**
- ▸ **Self-esteem**
- ▸ **Bullying**
- ▸ **Positive Behaviour Management**
- ▸ **Circle Time**
- ▸ **Anger Management**
- ▸ **Asperger's Syndrome**
- ▸ **Eating Disorders**